This book belongs to

CLEMENT C. MOORE

THE NIGHT BEFORE CHRISTMAS

Pictures by
GYO FUJIKAWA

GROSSET & DUNLAP · PUBLISHERS · NEW YORK

ISBN 0-448-02935-9 (TRADE)
ISBN 0-448-03181-7 (LIBRARY)

'Twas the night before Christmas,
    when all through the house
Not a creature was stirring,
    not

                even

                        a

                            mouse;

The stockings were hung
by the chimney with care,
In hopes that St. Nicholas
soon would be there;

The children were nestled all snug in their beds,

While visions of sugar-plums danced in their heads;

And Mamma in her 'kerchief,
   and I in my cap,
Had just settled our brains
   for a long winter's nap,

When out on the lawn
   there arose such a clatter,
I sprang from the bed
   to see what was the matter.

Away to the window
   I flew like a flash,
Tore open the shutters
   and threw up the sash.

The moon on the breast
   of the new-fallen snow
Gave the luster of midday
   to objects below,

When,
what to my wondering eyes
   should appear,

But a miniature sleigh,
   and eight tiny reindeer,

With a little old driver,
   so lively and quick,
I knew in a moment
   it must be St. Nick.

More rapid than eagles
his coursers they came,
And he whistled, and shouted,
and called them by name:

"Now, *Dasher!* now, *Dancer!*
  now, *Prancer* and *Vixen!*
On, *Comet!* on, *Cupid!*
  on, *Donder* and *Blitzen!*

To the top of the porch!
  to the top of the wall!
Now dash away! dash away!
  dash away all!''

As dry leaves that before
the wild hurricane fly,
When they meet with an obstacle,
mount to the sky,

So up to the housetop
  the coursers they flew,
With the sleigh full of toys,
  and St. Nicholas, too.

And then, in a twinkling,
  I heard on the roof
The prancing and pawing
  of each little hoof.

As I drew in my head,
    and was turning around,
Down the chimney St. Nicholas
    came with a bound.

He was dressed all in fur,
    from his head to his foot,
And his clothes were all tarnished
    with ashes and soot;

A bundle of toys
    he had flung on his back,
And he looked like a peddler
    just opening his pack.

His eyes — how they twinkled!
　　his dimples how merry!
His cheeks were like roses,
　　his nose like a cherry!

His droll little mouth
　　　was drawn up like a bow,
And the beard on his chin
　　　was as white as the snow;

The stump of a pipe
　　　he held tight in his teeth,
And the smoke it encircled
　　　his head like a wreath;

He had a broad face
and a little round belly
That shook when he laughed,
like a bowlful of jelly.

He was chubby and plump,
a right jolly old elf,
And I laughed when I saw him,
in spite of myself;

A wink of his eye
and a twist of his head
Soon gave me to know
I had nothing to dread.

He spoke not a word,
      but went straight to his work,
And filled all the stockings;
      then turned with a jerk,

And laying his finger
      aside of his nose,
And giving a nod,
      up the chimney he rose;

He sprang to his sleigh,
      to his team gave a whistle,
And away they all flew
      like the down of a thistle.

But I heard him exclaim,
      ere he drove out of sight,

HAPPY CHRISTMAS
TO ALL AND TO ALL
A GOOD NIGHT."